I0149629

All Scripture references taken from the KJV of the Holy Bible, unless otherwise indicated.

Spiritual Thieves by Dr. Marlene Miles

Freshwater Press 2025

ISBN: 978-1-967860-10-4

Paperback Version

Table of Contents

Spiritual Thieves

Freshwater

Introduction

This book is based on the video: *Prayers Against Spiritual Thieves*, but covers many more subjects.

Prayers against *spiritual thieves* is conducted in the Courts of Heaven and there is a protocol to entering into the Courts and to the Throne of God. We first acknowledge and worship the Lord. Be sure you are saved. Next, we ask the Lord to convene a Court. There are several different courts so be sure you are going to the right one for the type of case that you want heard. Ask the Holy Spirit to guide you.

In Court you present your case using the Word of God, therefore you will find in this prayer and in this book, there are many uses of Scripture. You don't have to know the Bible by heart, but use the Book and find the verses that you need. Do that before you go, as you prepare your case. As you pray, additional verses may come to mind. Stop and look those verses up and use them. This is another way to learn the Bible and that is by using the Bible.

Jesus is your Advocate.

If you've been accused, yes, you are guilty, and the Blood of Jesus is your defense. Ask the Lord for what you want. You want a Divine Judgment against the enemy and you want the case to go in your favor.

If you are returning to the Courts of Heaven because you already won a case but the enemy is still bothering you, oppressing you, attacking you, or stealing from you, then say that. Remind the Court of the previous verdict and report that it is not being followed and the offender needs to be dealt with by Heaven.

No one can do this for you, although I've heard pastors say they are opening up a case for you. As the shepherd of a local congregation he can stand for a corporate body, but it would behoove you to learn how to go into the Courts of Heaven yourself.

The Word of God says that we can come boldly. So, you see, we are invited, and we have a place there.

Let us therefore come boldly to the throne of grace, that we may obtain mercy and find grace to help in time of need. (Hebrews 4:16 NKJV)

Saints of God, another can priest for us at an altar, but if you are going into the Courts of Heaven, Jesus is your lawyer. You are not taking anyone with you. Yes, we are surrounded by a cloud of witnesses for a reason. Someone is always watching and taking notes, so we must walk circumspectly in life. But when you go before the Lord, you go, yourself.

Let your case be heard. Receive the verdict of the Righteous Judge, be thankful and worshipful.

This book is about spiritual thieves; we are warring in the spirit realm in the Courts of Heaven; we are not fighting against people but more the powers that drive and empower them to do the evil that they do. Going against the spiritual thieves is a better way since one *spirit* or evil entity may influence more than one person, even as many people as possible to torment or take from you. Surely you know people who have in exasperation said, *Why does it seem that people always want to take, take, take from me?*

In this quest we are asking for more than just physical tangible things, we are also asking return of things such as joy and peace. My book, **Among Some Thieves** addresses this issue differently in that it deals with thieves in the natural and all the things they impact and steal. That book also has some prayer points.

In this book, **<u>Spiritual Thieves</u>**, prayer points are enumerated but pray and say the Scriptures, they are part of your case presentation in the Courts of the Lord. The whole Psalms are not enumerated as not to confuse the real verse numbers as found in the Bible.

This book is divided into sections or chapters for ease of reading, praying, especially when used to pray together with another or in a group so you can all stay on the same prayer points. Enumerated prayer points are only available in the printed versions of this book.

Psalm 8

O Lord, our Lord how excellent is thy name in all the earth! who has set thy glory above the heavens. Out of the mouth of babes and sucklings, hast thou ordained strength because of thine enemies.

That thou mightest still the enemy and the avenger. When I consider thy heavens, the work of thy fingers, the moon and the stars which thou hast ordained. What is man that thou art mindful of him and the son of man that thou visitest him?

For thou has made him a little lower than the angels and hast crowned him with glory and honour. Thou madest him to have dominion over the works of thy hands, thou hast put all things

under his feet. All sheep and oxen yea,
and the beasts of the field.

The fowl of the air and the fish of the
sea and whatsoever passeth through
the paths of the seas.

O Lord, our Lord how excellent is thy
name in all the earth!

Repentance

1. Lord, have Mercy on me, a sinner. If I am none of Yours, give me a Godly sorrow and a repentant heart for my sins.

2. Hear my prayers of confession and make me one of Yours. I believe that Jesus is the Son of God and that He came to Earth and died on the Cross. And, on the third day He was resurrected, and He lives. Amen.

3. And I believe and I confess, and therefore I am saved, in the Name of Jesus.

4. Lord, have Mercy on me, have Mercy on me, Son of David, have Mercy on me. Lord, show Mercy to my parents and ancestors and forgive the iniquity of our bloodline all the way back to

Adam and Eve, where I also retrieve my essence, in the Name of Jesus.

5. Lord, I repent for every sin, I renounce and denounce the sin and ask that the Blood of Jesus cover me and remove my iniquity, so that there is nothing in me that the enemy can latch onto against me, in the Name of Jesus.

6. Lord, I repent for every sin, I renounce and denounce the sin, the transgression and I ask that the Blood of Jesus cover me and remove my iniquity, so there is nothing in me that the enemy can hold onto, so that no curse will alight, in the Name of Jesus.

7. Lord, we all have sinned and fallen short of the glory of God. Therefore, I plead the Blood of Jesus, the Blood of Jesus, the Blood of Jesus. Lord, see me through the Blood of Jesus. Jesus, my Righteousness, in the Name of Jesus.

Psalm 59

Deliver me, Lord, from mine enemies.
Oh my God, defend me. From them that
rise up against me, deliver me from the
workers of iniquity, and save me from
bloody men.

For lo, they lie in wait for my soul, the
mighty are gathered against me, not for
my transgression, nor for my sin. Oh
Lord, they run and prepare themselves
without my fault. Awake to help me.
And behold thou therefore, O, Lord God
of hosts, the God of Israel awake to visit
all the heathen. Be not merciful to any
wicked transgressors. Selah

They return at evening. They make a
noise like a dog and go round about the
city. Behold, they belch out with their
mouth. Swords are in their lips, for who
say they don't hear?

But thou, O Lord, shall laugh at them,
Thou shalt have all the heathen in
derision because of his strength. Will I

wait upon thee, for God is my defense, the God of my mercy shall prevent me. God shall let me see my desire upon mine enemies.

Slay them not, lest my people forget. Scatter them by thy power, and bring them down. O Lord, our shield for the sin of their mouth and the words of their lips, let them even be taken in their pride. And for cursing and lying which they speak. Consume them in wrath, consume them that they may not be, and let them know that God ruleth in Jacob unto the ends of the earth, Selah.

And at evening let them return, and let them make a noise like a dog, and go round about the city. Let them wander up and down for meat and grudge if they be not satisfied.

But I will sing of thy power. Yay, I will sing aloud of thy mercy in the morning, for thou hast been my defense and refuge in the day of my trouble. Unto Thee, O, my strength will I sing. For God is my defense, and the God of my mercy. Amen.

Courts of Heaven

8. Lord, I come to Your Throne in the Courts of Judgments tonight, in the Name of Jesus, asking You to hear my case and make a Divine Judgment in my favor regarding spiritual thieves, spiritual thievery, spiritual thefts against me and my bloodline, Lord, I come, in the Name of Jesus.

9. I am in Christ. I am the righteousness of God, in Christ Jesus. I am in Christ.

10. Lord, my family is saved and serving the Lord to the best of our spiritual ability and knowledge; help me. Help us, in the Name of Jesus.

11. But Lord, there is a thief. Maybe a pack of thieves, because
the thief cometh not, but to steal, and to kill and to destroy. And I am come

that they may have life, and they may have it more abundantly. (John 10:10)

12. But Lord, there are things missing from my life, and Jesus came that I would have life and have it more abundantly.

13. Thank You Jesus; I have life, I move, I breathe, I have being, in the Name of Jesus. But where is my abundance?

14. I may not have seen you, thief, but like a thief in the night, I know what you did, and I know that what is for me is for me. What is mine is mine, so you must take your hands off what is mine, in Jesus' Name.

15. Lord, I present to the Court that my abundance is missing because it's been stolen by a thief.

16. Also, other things are missing, such as my joy, my peace, and the things that belong to my peace.

17. Abundance is mine. That means I should have more than enough, more

than enough to share with others in need. But it's missing.

18. And whatever else is missing that's been stolen by the thief, I present to the Court that I need returned to me:

- my health
- my strength
- my marriage
- my children
- my success,
- my awards
- my promotions
- my accomplishments
- my favor
- my education
- my certificates
- my appreciation
- my boldness
- my confidence
- my garment
- my glory, the glory due to man
- my crown
- my star
- my dominion

- my scepter
- my power
- my light
- my ambition
- my career
- my business, my businesses
- my finances
- my savings
- my retirement
- my house
- my houses
- my investments
- my car
- my hope
- school funds
- vacation funds

19. Lord, I may not know all, but I know if things are not right and if I have no job where I should have a job, I am educated or properly trained and experienced, then the thief is involved in my not having a job. I report it now to Heaven in this Court, in the Name of Jesus.

20. Lord, if I have a job but it is far beneath me, the thief is at work.

21. If my diplomas and certificates have been stolen or rendered ineffective or tampered with, rendered useless, that is more work of the Thief. I bind that witchcraft from further working against me and I dismantled the evil covenant and the spell that allows it. East Wind of God blow that curse away and the one who sent it, in the Name of Jesus.

22. Father, no matter what job I have, but if I work and have little to no money, the thief is at work and I report to Heaven and ask for speedy righteous judgment to remedy this matter, in the Name of Jesus.

23. And, Lord, if I work and I don't have any money, I report to Heaven. And in this court right now, hear my plea, Lord, hear my petition and honor my words and my presentation. I am in Christ and He is my Advocate.

Not A Slave

24. Father, I'm a bond servant of Christ.

    I am not a slave.

    I am not a slave.

    I am not a slave to sin.

25. Father, if there's a secret or secret sin or a hidden sin that's hidden to me, show it to me that I may repent and be freed of it and its iniquity, in the Name of Jesus.

26. I am not a slave to sin.

27. I am not a slave to iniquity.

28. I am not a slave to bondage.

29. I am not shackled.

30. I'm not padlocked, chained, roped, tied, or yoked, in the Name of Jesus.

31. I am not a slave, and I do not work for free. I do not work for little. I do not work for nothing, in the Name of Jesus.

32. Instead, Lord, those things that have been stolen from me have been replaced by false things, counterfeit things by the thief.

33. I reject any counterfeit blessings or inferior substitutes that the thief has offered, given, or placed anywhere near me or in my possession, in the Name of Jesus.

34. Lord, forgive me if I have inadvertently accepted anything from this liar, this thief, in the Name of Jesus.

35. Holes in pockets made by the thief be healed, be mended, in the Name of Jesus.

36. Wealth siphoned off of me. Lord, stop the leakage and return all my possessions back to me, in the Name of Jesus.

37. Household thieves, stand down, repent and be saved. Change your wicked ways, or receive the wrath of God.

38. Thou shalt not suffer a witch to live, (Exodus 22:18)

39. Holes in hands where money mysteriously goes away or leaks out be healed and sealed by the Blood of Jesus, and never to leak again in Jesus' Name.

Spiritual Thieves

40. Spiritual thieves, spiritual wickedness, spiritual entities inspiring and empowering thievery against me, I have no Mercy for you.

41. According to the Word of God, he who steals shall surely die.

42. Spiritual thieves, die, die, die, Lose your power against me, in the Name of Jesus.

43. Lord, if the thief be found breaking in and be smitten, and if he dies, there shall be no bloodshed for him.

44. If a man shall steal an ox or a sheep to kill it or sell it, he shall restore five oxen for an ox, and four sheep for a sheep. (Exodus 22:2-3)

45. The thief cometh not but to steal, kill, and destroy. But I am come that they might have life, and have it more abundantly, says the Word of God.

46. Lord, let him who steals, steal no more, let him that stole steal no more, no more for me, but rather let him labor working with his hands, the thing which is good, that he may have to give to him that needed. (Ephesians 4:28)

47. Lord, let any and every entity and their evil human agents that stole from me be no more able to steal from me again, in the Name of Jesus.

48. Bind their hands, bind their minds, confound their plans, bind their altars, bind their powers, bind them so they are ineffective and powerless against me, in the Name of Jesus.

49. Lord, dislodge them from my life, from my life, from my life. Dislodge them from my gates, dislodge them from my places of prosperity and from

my staff of bread, in the Name of Jesus.

50. Lord, I have repented, and the iniquity is removed; let them steal from me no more. Let the curse not alight here anymore, in the Name of Jesus.

51. Lord, hide me under the shadow of the wings of the Most High, so I cannot be located in the Spirit, in the Name of Jesus. Thank You, Lord.

Do Not Let Me Steal

And thou therefore which teaches another, teaches thou not thyself? thou that preaches that man should not steal dost thou steal? (Romans 2:21)

52. Lord, let me not steal, let me not be a thief, so I do not attract the same to my life in any way, in the Name of Jesus.

53. Let me not be a thief, Lord, so I do not hate my own soul, in the Name of Jesus.

54. Whoso is a partner with the thief hateth his own soul; he heareth, cursing and bewrayeth it not. (Proverbs 29:24)

Restitution

And if a man shall steal an ox or sheep and kill it, or sell it, he shall restore five oxen for an ox and for a sheep, four sheep. (Exodus 22:1)

55. Lord, any thief who stole from the flocks of my field, or from the works of my hand, that entity and or his *representative* in the Earth must repay fivefold for the work oxen, fourfold for the sheep, in the Name of Jesus. Thank You, Lord.

56. Thou shalt not steal. Thou shalt not steal from God's anointed. Do no harm to God's anointed. Touch not His anointed and to His prophet do no harm, in the Name of Jesus.

57. And I despise the thief, Lord. I hate him with perfect hate, in the Name of Jesus, because he did not steal to eat or to satisfy his soul because he's hungry. He stole because he's a thief. And he comes not but to steal, kill and destroy. (Proverbs 6:30)

58. Lord, I ask for Divine Judgement against the thief and his co- thieves or other independent thieves working against me from any evil altar, in the Name of Jesus.

59. Men do not despise a thief if he steals to satisfy my soul when he is hungry. But you shall not steal or deal falsely nor lie to one another.

60. Lord, as You are against the thieves, murderers, adulterers, those who swear falsely and burn incense to Baal and walk after other *gods*, I am also against them, in the Name of Jesus. Will you steal, murder and commit adultery and swear, and burn incense to Baal and walk after other *gods* whom you do not know? (Jeremiah 7:9)

61. I report to Heaven: Lord, that I've been robbed or burgled or lied upon, cheated, cheated out of opportunities, promotions, divine connections, and I want them back now, in the Name of Jesus.

62. Lord, have Your Angels search the land of the living and the dead, and return these stolen things to me, snatching them out of the hands of the thieves, if necessary, in the Name of Jesus.

63. And I break up every evil network of thieves and their network of evil altars by the Thunder Hammer of God. And the power of the Blood of Jesus.

64. Multiple networks of evil working against me, especially to steal from me. I break you by the power in the Blood of Jesus.

65. And I break up every evil network of thieves. I break up their network of evil altars by the Thunder Hammer of

God, by the power in the Blood of Jesus.

66. Multiple networks of evil working against me, especially to steal from me. I break you by the power in the blood of Jesus.

67. Automatic networks of evil working against me, I return your spells, curses, hexes, vexes, and incantations. I return them back to you with immediacy and speed, in the Name of Jesus.

68. Multiple networks of evil working against me, especially to steal from me, I break you by the power in the Blood of Jesus.

69. Automatic networks of evil working against me, I return your spells, curses, hexes, vexes and incantations back to you with immediacy and power and speed, in the Name of Jesus.

70. Thank You, Lord.

Heavenly Treasures

71. Father, I will not lay up for myself treasure in Earth, where moth and rust doth corrupt and thieves can break into steal. But Lord, instead I lay up for myself treasures in Heaven, where neither moth nor rust corrupt, and where thieves do not break through or steal, in the Name of Jesus.

72. Father, thank You for the true riches, but tonight I speak of tangible and also intangible things that have been stolen from me, things that pertain to my peace, things that pertain to my life and my godliness. And I ask for a Divine Judgment against the thieves and for those items that have been stolen to be returned to me, multiplied

according to the Word of God, in the Name of Jesus. Thank You, Lord.

73. I do know the commandments and I speak loudly in the Spirit. Do not commit adultery, do not kill, do not steal, do not bear false witness, do not defraud, and also do honor your father and mother.

74. Thank You, Lord, that You grace me with the true riches--, incorruptible, Godly, true riches that cannot be stolen.

75. But Father, I'm making mention and petition of those things needed for living here in this Earth realm, that have been taken from me, in the Name of Jesus. They must be returned. Amen.

76. Lord, forgive me for any lack of wisdom if I have not put what is mine safely away or if I have not exhibited wise stewardship. Lord, if I have not used bags that are not old, forgive me and redeem back to me anything lost,

dropped, or left carelessly, or anything easily stolen, in the Name of Jesus.

77. Thank You, Lord.

Sell what you have, give alms, provide yourselves bags which wax not old. A treasure in the heavens that faileth not where no thief approaches, neither moth corrupteth. (Luke 12:33)

78. Lord, forgive me for any idolatry toward anything that was stolen from me, and if it was Divine Judgment that caused the loss, Lord, please forgive me and remove the judgment and also the iniquity, so that I may live again in Christ, in the Name of Jesus, and to the praise of Your glory.

79. Lord, I speak of those things that are enough for me, even more than enough, even abundance prescribed for me long ago for my purpose, for my station and position on Earth--, those things needed for life and for godliness, in the Name of Jesus.

80. Lest I be full and denied thee, or say, who is the Lord, or lest I be poor and steal and take the name of my God in vain. (Proverbs 30:9)

God's Anointed

81. Lord, in the Name of Jesus, I call for judgment against any entity that would dare steal from a servant of the Lord, any that would dare steal from a person who abides in Christ. How would they steal that silver and gold?

82. Behold, the money which we found in our sack's mouth, we brought again unto thee out of the land of Canaan. How then should we steal out of the Lord's house silver or gold?

83. Lord, I proclaim that all silver, gold, money, things of value, everything of value that has been stolen from me must be returned because it was stolen from a person who is in Christ, in the Name of Jesus.

84. Lord, let the natural man that stole steal no more, but rather let him labor, working with his hands the thing which is good, that he may have to give to him that needeth. Amen.

85. Spiritual thieves, coveting devils, demons, imps, unclean *spirits*, lying and thieving *spirits*, you have been found out. Loose your hold on everything that is mine. Drop it and give it back to me, in the Name of Jesus.

86. Lord, that is my request in this Court tonight, in the Name of Jesus, that what has been stolen from me will be returned fivefold, fourfold, doubled, even up to seven-fold, even if it spoils the strong man's house, in the Name of Jesus.

87. And, Lord let me be stolen from no more, in the Name of Jesus.

But let none of you suffer as a murderer, or as a thief, or as an evildoer, or as a busybody in other men's matters. (1 Peter 4:15)

88. I do not join in with thieves and adulterers. (Psalm 50:18)

89. I do not belong to a ring of thieves, and neither should I ever be ripped off by them, in the Name of Jesus.

90. Lord, I know that:
If a thief be found breaking in, and he be smitten that he die, there shall no blood be shed for him. (Exodus 22:2)

91. If a man shall deliver unto is neighbour money or stuff to keep, and it be stolen out of the man's house; if the thief be found, let him pay double. (Exodus 22:7)

92. If it is stolen from that neighbors' house and that thief is found he shall pay double. If he steals a **man** and **sells the man** and if he be found in his hand or possession, he shall be put to death.

93. And he that stealeth a man, and selleth him, or if he be found in his

hand, he shall surely be put to death.
(Exodus 21:16)

94. Anyone or anything, any entity that has ever stolen anything of mine or anything of *me, including* any part of me and sold me, **let that power die**. Let it die. Let that entity surely be put to death according to the Word of God, in Exodus 21:16 and 22:7, in the Name of Jesus.

...cargoes of cinnamon and spice, of incense, myrrh and frankincense, of wine and olive oil, of fine flour and wheat; cattle and sheep; horses and carriages; and human beings sold as slaves. (Revelation 18:13 NIV)

95. Entities and powers that deal in the selling of men's souls–, the LORD Jesus rebuke you, 24/7.

96. If a man be found stealing any of his brethren of the children of Israel, and maketh merchandise of him, or selleth him; then that thief shall die; and thou shalt put evil away from among you. (Deuteronomy 24:7)

97. If any part of my body is being used against my knowledge and against my

will in covens or in spiritual realms in any way, the Lord Jesus Christ rebuke the perpetrator(s). Father, have Your Mighty Angels rescue me and deliver me, bring me out of this captivity, in the Name of Jesus.

98. Lord, if I have been taken in the natural for any reason, save me, deliver me, in the Name of Jesus.

99. Father, let my voice be heard and echo in the spirit, when I say to the enemy: I am not your candidate for sin, for evil, for trafficking, for slavery or sacrifice of any kind, in the Name of Jesus.

100. Lord, let my voice be heard in the spirit when I say to the enemy: Neither my children, my spouse, nor my family is not your candidate for sin, for evil, for trafficking, for slavery, or sacrifice of any kind, in the Name of Jesus.

101. Lord, if any part of my being, my soul, or my humanity has been stolen

and either held captive or used in any nefarious, any evil way, Father, have Your Angels separate my humanity from any synthetic or evil composition and return my humanity to me, so that I am made whole again, in the Name of Jesus.

102. Lord, if I have been sold, buy me back, buy me back, buy me back from wherever they have sold me, in the Name of Jesus.

103. Lord, if any part of my soul has been sold, after being stolen, buy me back, buy me back, in the Name of Jesus.

104. Any part of my soul that has been stolen in sudden devastation, trauma, shock, awe, or sudden destruction, Lord, send Your Angels to look for me. Search the land of the living and the dead and find my lost humanity that I am returned safe and sound and made whole again, in the Name of Jesus.

105.   Lord, forgive. Son of David, have Mercy on me, forgive. Forgive my sin and iniquity by the Blood of Jesus.

106.   Lord, if any part of me or my soul has been stolen due to sin, rebellion, disobedience, ignorance, arrogance, or just stupidity, Lord, have Your Angels search the land of the living and the dead to bring me back and restore my soul, make me whole, in the Name of Jesus. Amen.

Return of Property

107. Whoever **steals** an ox or a sheep and slaughters it or sells it must pay back five head of cattle for the ox and four sheep for the sheep. (Exodus 22)

108. Lord, any thief who has stolen anything from me that has to do with my livelihood or staff of bread must pay back at least fivefold for what he stole, in the Name of Jesus.

109. If a thief is caught breaking in at night and is struck a fatal blow, the defender is not guilty of bloodshed; (Exodus 22:2A)

110. Of spiritual thieves, Lord, let them die the death, in the Name of Jesus. (X3, or more.)

111. Lord, have Your Mighty Warrior Angels deal accordingly with thieves

that break in like those who sow tares at night when I am unaware or in the dream state, deal with them strongly, in the Name of Jesus.

112.   I ask that a Divine Judgment be rendered in my favor, in the Name of Jesus. Father, render a Divine Judgment against spiritual thieves, in the Name of Jesus.

Restitution

113.   Anyone who steals must certainly make restitution, but if they have nothing, *they* must be sold to pay for their theft.

114.   If the stolen animal is found alive in their possession, whether ox or donkey or sheep, they must pay back double.

115.   Lord, anything stolen from me must be repaid double for my trouble at the very least. Some fivefold, some fourfold, some sevenfold.

116.   Jesus said if the sheep thief be found out they must make restitution, in the Name of Jesus.

117.   If anyone grazes their livestock in a field or vineyard and lets them stray

and they graze in someone else's field, the offender must make restitution from the best of their own field or vineyard.

118.   Father if anyone is using what is mine to make profit, to make money, if any thief is sneaking in and using what is mine, whether they outrightly take it out of my possession or if they sneakily just use it to benefit themselves and I'm not benefiting and they don't have permission to do it, Lord, that is a THIEF. Deal with them accordingly, in the Name of Jesus.

119.   That thief is found out, they must make restitution to me, in the Name of Jesus.

120.   Lord, have the thief repay me the very best they have for what they took from me; if that's an upgrade for me, then so be it, according to Exodus 22:6, in the Name of Jesus.

121.   Father, if this thief does not present himself or herself to answer for this

thievery, then according to Exodus 22:7, the **owner of the house** must appear before the judges. Lord, You are the Righteous Judge. They must present before You so it may be determined whether the owner of the house has laid hands on the other person's property. (Exodus 22:7)

122.   Father, You are the Righteous Judge. Wherever and from whomever this thief got their power to steal from me, I am calling the place where they got their evil power, the *owner of the house*. If needs be, Father, spoil that house, spoil that strongman, spoil the owner, spoil that power, spoil them, for Your servant's sake, in the Name of Jesus.

123.   Judge righteously, Lord. Rule with Your Rod of Iron, Lord, and spoil them, in the Name of Jesus.

124.   In all cases of illegal possession of an ox, a donkey, a sheep, a garment, or any other lost property about which somebody says, 'This is mine,'

both parties are to bring their cases before the judges.(Exodus 22:9)

125. I bring my case, Lord, respectfully and honorably to the Righteous Judge, the Judge of all mankind, the Judge of the Universe.

126. I am here in this Court and at this Throne Lord, because the enemy has stolen what is mine from me, and I demand it back from him or them. I demand it. I demand it, in the Name of Jesus. (Exodus 22:9)

127. The one whom the Judge declares guilty must pay back double to the other, according to the Word of God.

128. Lord, I ask for Divine Judgment against my adversary, against the thief and I require no less than double for my trouble, and I put a time stamp on that restitution of **IMMEDIATELY**, with expediency, with immediacy, in the Name of Jesus.

Exodus 22:18

129.   Lord, in the middle of this chapter in Exodus, it reads, **Suffer not a witch to live.** (Exodus 22:18). Thieving witches, lose your power, lose your power, lose your power against me, in the Name of Jesus.

130.   Whatever you have taken, time, joy, opportunities, relationships, success, money, promotions, health, strength, life, children, you must return it. Lord, we do not wrestle against flesh and blood, but judge the powers that embolden and empower the evil human agents against the people of God, in the Name of Jesus.

131.   Judge the evil *house* behind the evil acts, in the Name of Jesus.

132. WHATEVER YOU STOLE FROM ME. What I know about and things I don't even know about. Must be returned with restitution, in the Name of Jesus.

133. Tangible things and intangible things. I know that I'm missing something. I KNOW I've been ripped off. I know that I am at a loss. I know there are things that I used to have that I don't now have, Father. I may not know what everything is, but I am putting in a claim for everything in this Court, in the Name of Jesus.

134. The things I know about, the things I don't know about, the things that I don't yet know about. I'm putting in a claim for everything, in the Name of Jesus.

135. Lord, have the thief return to me everything that has been stolen from me since my birth, in the Name of Jesus.

136. Lord, have the thicf return to me the things stolen from my bloodline, since time immemorial, in the Name of Jesus.

Sneaking Thieves

137.   I know the Thief has been coming into the sheepfold.

138.   Verily, verily, I say unto you, He that entereth not by the door into the sheepfold, but climbeth up some other way, the same is a thief and a robber. (John 10:1)

139.   Anybody who snuck into my life, anybody who snuck into my business or into my environment and they came in sneakily, stealthily by some other way than straight up and through the door; they are the thief (John 10:1)

140.   They shall run to and fro in the city; they shall run upon the wall, they shall climb up upon the houses; they shall enter in at the windows like a thief. (Joel 2:9)

141.   If they came in some other way;
        that is the thief, that is the thief, in the
        Name of Jesus.

142.   Thieves who snuck in to lead silly
        women astray, the Lord Jesus rebuke
        you.

For of this sort are they which creep into
    houses, and lead captive silly women
    laden with sins, led away with divers
            lusts (2 Timothy 3:6)

143.   Lord, as a man, You have made me
        a   protector   of   women,   not   an
        opportunist against them. Forgive me
        if I have ever taken advantage of
        women instead of properly looking
        out for them as You have established,
        in the Name of Jesus.

144.   Lord,   as   a   female,   give   me
        Wisdom and the Mind of Christ so that
        I am not a silly woman, in the Name
        of Jesus.

145.   Thief: Whether I knew you or not.

146.   Whether I trusted you or not.

147.   Whether you lied to me, whether you tricked me, no matter how this robbery came to be, I call you out. The Lord Jesus rebuke you and render judgment against you, in the Name of Jesus.

148.   Whether you snuck through a window or some other opening that was not the door, you are a thief, and you must answer to this Court, in the Name of Jesus.

149.   Whether I noticed it or not, even if I was ignorant of it, I call you out, I call you THIEF, this day, I call you out and I demand you return to me all that is mine in multiples, in multiplicity according to the Word of God. Now, in the Name of Jesus.

150.   Even if you tricked me and I gave you the **BAG**: I call you out now, and I say return to me, according to the Word of God, all that was stolen from me, in the Name of Jesus.

151.   Speaking of JUDAS:

This he said, not that he cared for the poor; but because he was a thief, and had the bag, and bare what was put therein.(John 12:6)

152. He was carrying what was in the bag. Even if you tricked me and I gave you the bag, I call you out now and I say you must return to me everything you stole from me, in the Name of Jesus.

153. Even if you were a family member, even if you were a friend, even if you were a trusted friend, even if you were a fake friend. Even if I gave you the bag to hold, to borrow, to use, and you didn't give back what you were supposed to give back, or you think I don't know you took it, by the power in the Blood of Jesus whatever power is influencing you or empowering you to steal from me, Lord, break that power, in the Name of Jesus.

154. Thank You, Lord.

Give Your Cloak

155.   Father, in the New Testament, Jesus said:
And if any man will sue thee at the law, and take away thy coat, let him have thy cloak also. (Matthew 5:40)

156.   Thank You, Lord for Jesus and for the Word of Truth.

157.   Thank You, Lord, for the Holy Spirit so that we may rightly divide this Word, in the Name of Jesus.

158.   A coat or a cloak--, there you go. I do not give the true riches away, in the Name of Jesus.

159.   I do not sit still if things of great value are being stolen, in the Name of Jesus.

- Peace

- Joy
- Fruits of the Spirit
- Destiny
- Purpose
- Spiritual Gifts
- Family
- Marriage – the greatest of all covenants
- Spouse
- Relationships
- Career
- Education
- Livelihood – staff of bread
- Birthright
- Inheritance
- Home
- Soul

160. Father, I refuse to sit idly by while the thief steals, kills, and destroys, but I ask that You render judgment, and help me, in the Name of Jesus.

I Do Not Forgive Them

161.   Lord, treat the thief like a thief.
Treat the thief like a thief, in the Name
of Jesus.

162.   The Word says in the New
Testament, that whose sins I forgive
are forgiven. I do not forgive the
thieves of the spirit; I do not forgive
them. Spiritual thieves in the spirit,
spiritual thieves. I do not forgive them.

If you forgive anyone's sins, their sins
are forgiven; if you do not forgive them,
they are not forgiven. (John 20:23)

Jesus also said, Father, forgive
them, for they know not what they do.
Jesus said that we should forgive people
70 X 7, even in a day. Saints of God, **Jesus**

came to Earth to forgive. Jesus never picked up a sword during His Earth ministry, although the Lord is a warrior, the Lord is His name. Also, Jesus is the Captain of the Host of the Armies of the Lord.

I, personally am in Christ, as are the saved, amen. But I am a spiritual warrior, and I do warfare. I pick up a sword daily. I sleep with a sword.

Let me share that with you, one night as I was lying in bed to sleep I had a vision of a sword there with me, so all I had to do was reach my hand there and the handle of it was there for me. It was a season of warfare, even in my sleep state and dreams, therefore the Lord knew that I needed it with me 24/7.

The Word of God is sharper than any two-edged sword. Do you not wield it, also? In reality, Jesus is the Word, the Word is the Sword, so why would Jesus need to pick up a dull, physical, man-made sword, when He **is** the real thing?

Furthermore, spiritual thieves ultimately cannot be forgiven, and they cannot be redeemed, so it would be foolish to try to forgive what God won't forgive when it is all said and done.

Nowhere in Scripture have I read that we are to forgive spiritual thieves. They cannot claim that they don't know what they are doing, they do know. They have been doing the same stealing, killing, and destroying for thousands of years; they know. And, I do **not** forgive them.

163. Like the soldiers who came out to lay hands on Jesus, LORD, have Your Mighty Warrior Angels lay hold to the strongmen, the thieves, the entities, the powers that steal from me or have stolen from me. Apprehend them, in the Name of Jesus.

164. In that same hour said Jesus to the multitudes, Are ye come out as against a thief with swords and staves for to take me? I sat daily with you teaching in the temple, and ye laid no hold on me. (Matthew 26:55)

165. Lord, as the natural authorities do lay hands on thieves, coming out with swords and staves, Lord, arise and come and rescue me from these strongmen, these thieves, these entities, and powers that steal. Lay hands on these spiritual thieves. Have Your Angels to lay hands on them as thieves because they are thieves, in the Name of Jesus.

166. I file my report to Heaven that I am missing things that pertain to my peace, my life, my godliness, my ministry, and my destiny, and I seek a Divine Judgment against these thieves, as well as restitution, in the Name of Jesus.

167. If the thief be not found, then the master of the house shall be brought unto the judges, to see whether he have put his hand unto his neighbor's goods. (Exodus 22:8)

168. The powers that are influencing them, the powers that are enforcing the

theft or empowering the thieves in the Earth realm, spiritual thieves and arranging and organizing them, and being invoked at their altars, let them be judged, by the Righteous Judge, in the Name of Jesus.

169.   Lord, You are Sovereign and you are supreme, let every evil verdict and judgment rendered against me by evil courts be made null and void, in the Name of Jesus.

170.   Lord, judge the satanic, witchcraft covens and all other evil courts making unrighteous judgments against me, in the Name of Jesus.

Collective Thievery

When I would have healed Israel, then
the iniquity of Ephraim was discovered,
and the wickedness of Samaria: for they
commit falsehood; and the thief cometh
in, and the troop of robbers spoileth
without. (Hosea 7:1)

171. Lord, forgive me, forgive my
people, my bloodline--, whatever
collective I am in that allowed this
captivity and this thievery, Lord,
forgive my town, city, even my nation
if necessary to redeem us from all of
this thievery and robbery and being
ripped off, in the Name of Jesus.

Then Jesus said unto the chief priests,
and captains of the temple, and the
elders, which were come to him, Be ye
come out as against a thief, with swords
and staves? (Luke 22:52)

172. Lord, deal with them as thieves, in the Name of Jesus.

173. Just as they laid hands on Jesus as if He was a thief and he was not – Lord, have Your Warrior Angels lay hands on these spiritual thieves, bind them, make them repay up to 7-fold for all they have taken , and then take them away, Dislodge them from the gates of my life and the gates of my family and proclaim, Failed assignment over them, in the Name of Jesus.

The Watch

But know this, that if the goodman of
the house had known in what watch the
thief would come, he would have
watched, and would not have suffered
his house to be broken up. (Matthew
24:43)

174.   Father, had I known, Lord, I would
have watched, forgive me for not
watching.

175.   Forgive me for either sleeping or
being ignorant or disobedient or
rebellious.

176.   Lord, forgive my parents and
ancestors for the same and return to
me what is rightfully mine, by
birthright, by inheritance, by the gifts
and the blessings of God and by the
work and labor of my own hands;

return it to me, Lord, in the Name of Jesus.

177. Father, return to me by Righteous Judgment what is due me, taking it out of the hands of every spiritual thief, strongman, evil entity, and out of the hands of every evil human agent that is working for or with this thieving gang, in the Name of Jesus.

178. Father, even if what was taken from me was rightfully stolen, I am pleading the Blood of Jesus because I am in Christ. Blood of Jesus, cry me out of every judgment that is up against me, in the Name of Jesus.

179. Lord, I appeal to Your Mercy and Your Grace, and loving kindness toward me, in the Name of Jesus. Lord, see me through the Blood, I am redeemed by the Blood, in the Name of Jesus.

180. Amazing Grace, how sweet the sound. I once was lost, but now I'm found, in the Name of Jesus.

181. Return all that has been stolen from me back to me because I am redeemed, I am redeemed.

182. I am redeemed. I was lost. I may have been stolen, but I was lost, and I am now found. I am redeemed, and therefore the things that belong to my peace, the things that belong to my life and my godliness, those things must also be redeemed.

183. I am in Christ, in the Name of Jesus.

Ways the Devil Steals

Excerpted from the video message: ***Ways the Devil Steals Your Money.*** https://www.youtube.com/watch?v=237uJ96jK GI&lc=UgwFP0ZwHmbeoJdalMN4AaABAg

From the days of John the Baptist til now the kingdom of heaven suffereth violence, and the violent take it by force.
(Matthew 11:12)

We have stewardship over things in the Earth and we are responsible to take care of things and also to keep up with things. As well we should be growing, multiplying and increasing whatever has been placed in our care.

Fear is a way people are stolen from by the devil. People chase diagnoses, doctors, meds, supplements because they are afraid of being sick or getting sick.

Many times, money is spent that may not even need to be spent. Money is lost by missing work. By not going to work a person loses money, spends money, and are not making money if they don't have paid time off.

Memory loss, distractions, and forgetfulness, missing deadlines, forgetting to go places or getting to places at the wrong time can cost money.

False prophets and liars lead people astray and being in the wrong timeline can cost a lot more than money; but it can also cost money.

Blockers put you on the wrong path in life. If you keep repeating things that do not need to be repeated, you waste so much, including finances.

The devil puts you in the wrong path, or in the right place at the wrong time, or in the wrong place at the right time. This causes people to miss blessings. God commands a blessing in certain places or under certain conditions: when the people are one as in unity.

Which leads us to divorce; that's a big money grabber. How many times are you going to buy and set up house with all of it's expenses, furniture and the like, get divorced and then leave it? The devil is stealing from you. Get married and work it out; stay with the spouse of your youth. So, marry wisely and well the first time and be sure that neither of you are bringing a lot of ***spiritual*** *baggage* into the marriage. If you have spiritual baggage, get deliverance.

The devil creates hardships, disasters, breaks things. Sends human tormentors who not only irritate you but can physically break things that belong to you and then you're stuck with the bill for a broken appliance or a wrecked car that you lent to someone, for example.

Delays in getting jobs or finishing education cost opportunities and money acquisition. The devil can send bad customers or clients to your current business. The devil can put reproach on you, so you lose business. Hateful people writing bad reviews are some of his other tricks. He can put up obstacles to your working or working efficiently. He can place a covering cast over your business, so you are not even seen or found in the marketplace.

The devil is not more powerful than God. He is never more powerful than Christ in you, but he is not sleeping, and he is thinking up devilment all the time. So, you have to be wise and prayed up, and for best results connected to a House of real believers, prayer warriors, intercessors, and the other gifts of the Spirit.

Business owners, unless you have impeccable staff, you must keep your eyes on them at all times. Sometimes employees simply take products out of the store or establishment because they want to. Sometimes they give things completely away or give things away at a discount that you did not authorize. Sometimes they take money out of the cash register. Sometimes employees come to work, but don't do any work. Hourly staff can become clock riders, doing nothing at all that benefits the business, but their own personal stuff, playing on their phones, or even hiding and sleeping. I've seen all of these scenarios and so much more in the workplace. Many are proud of how little they do on their jobs.

Then there are the ones who say they can do things but they can't. So instead of making $25 an hour, they make $35 an hour and do $25 per hour level of work. That person is a liar and a thief, as well as all the others who do not earn their hire.

This is sad because the person who is cheating the employer is also cheating himself as well as setting up **iniquity** for their children and generations. First of all, the Word says who will give you what is your own if you don't take care of another's? Of a fact, there was a man with several children, but he was a lazy man who thought himself more clever than most. In the long run, his children who are bright and educated, do not have jobs, cannot keep jobs, and this writer believes it is because of the iniquity he created by disrespecting his own employers, when he even worked, over the years. He did not set a good example for them in the natural, but in the spirit, he sowed workplace and job **iniquity** that the children and also their children are paying as they suffer in their careers and financially.

Saints of God: reality check. We want our children to look like us. We want them to be like us. We even name them after ourselves as if we are some great monument or pillar of virtue and success, but then we don't want them to go through the trouble and the hardships that we have endured in life. Life is spiritual and that is another way of saying lives are connected, especially

those that share the same blood. So, how will your children be different than you, or have a different life than you have, unless you are now in Christ and your foundation is changed?

182. Lord, show me quickly and early any employee who is a liar and a thief, a clock rider, a do-nothing or a cheat, and give me Wisdom on how best to handle the situation, in the Name of Jesus.

Prayers Against Being Stolen From

183. We have done some spiritual Sherlocking and found that it is the devil behind negative things that are happening to us or positive things that should be happening but are not happening for us. Blessings that may have been misappropriated, stolen, taken away, channeled and funneled and shuffled over to the agents of the devil. This is why we are in the Courts of God, to seek a Divine Judgment against this adversary.

182. Holy Ghost Fire, fall now, in the Name of Jesus.

183. In the Name of Jesus, I come to You, Lord with true repentance, and an

offering, a sacrifice of Thanksgiving and praise.

184. Lord, I raise an altar to You, an altar of worship for You are God, and You are worthy of all my Thanksgiving and my praise.

185. In the Name of Jesus, I raise an altar to You, Lord, of a worthy offering, be it first fruits, tithes, and our offerings, in the Name of Jesus.

186. Because I love You Lord, I love God, I also I'm raising this offering so that my prayers will be heard, in the Name of Jesus.

187. Father, I repent of prayerlessness where I could have called a thousand Angels, but my mouth was closed.

188. Lord, forgive me.

189. Where I could have agreed with another person, at least one other, and put 10,000 Angels into action, into flight against the works of the devil, but I did not, either I did not open my

mouth or because I couldn't get along with my *brother* long enough even to agree in prayer.

190. Lord, forgive me. I repent of carelessness and prayerlessness, in the Name of Jesus.

191. I repent of having ought against my brother or sister. I repent of causing any hurt or ought against my brother or sister, in the Name of Jesus.

192. I regard no iniquity in my heart. Lord: hear my prayer, hear my petition.

193. Father, I repent of sleeping, and slumbering, and laziness.

194. I repent to partying and revelry and any work of the flesh, in the Name of Jesus.

195. I repent of robbing God, of robbing You, Lord, because You hate robbery, especially in offerings.

196. I repent of robbing any man, woman, any person, in the Name of Jesus.

197. I repent of hurting any man or woman or person, in the Name of Jesus.

198. I repent of any type of attack against any person, in the Name of Jesus, and Lord, if this has been written of me in the Spirit, I plead for Mercy, and I plead the Blood of Jesus.

199. I decree that by the Blood of Jesus I speak Grace, I speak deliverance, and I speak Peace.

200. By the power of the speaking Blood of Jesus, every work of darkness claiming legal ground in my life and family stands dislodged forever, in the Name of Jesus.

201. Father, I repent of being unthankful, I repent of entitlement, I repent of not opening my mouth with Thanksgiving so I may enter into the Gates of the Lord.

202. Father, I repent of not praising You. Lord, if the rocks have had to cry out in my stead because I didn't praise

You, please forgive me, in Jesus' Name.

203. I vow to praise You and worship You in the beauty of Your holiness.

204. Father, I repent of not honoring You in my sacrifices and tithes and offerings.

205. Father, I repent of any disobedience, rebellion, idolatry, witchcraft and even blind witchcraft.

206. Lord, forgive me of every sin known and unknown, seen and unseen, according to Your loving kindness.

207. Lord, have Mercy on me, have Mercy on me, O God, according to Your unfailing Love.

208. According to Your great compassion. Blot out my transgressions, wash away all my iniquity, and cleanse me from my sin, for I know my transgressions, and my sin is always before me.

209. Against You only have I sinned. Lord, I have done what is evil in Your sight, so You are right in Your verdict and justified when You judge.

210. Surely, I was sinful at birth, sinful from the time my mother conceived me. Yet You desired faithfulness even in the womb.

211. You taught me Wisdom in that secret place.

212. Cleanse me with hyssop and I shall be clean. Wash me, and I will be whiter than snow. Let me hear joy and gladness. Let the bones you have crushed rejoice.

213. Hide your face from my sins and blot out all my iniquity.

214. Create in me a pure heart, O God, and renew a steadfast spirit in me.

215. Do not cast me away from your presence or take Your Holy Spirit from me.

216. Restore to me the joy of Your salvation, and grant to me a willing spirit to sustain me.

217. Then will I teach transgressors Your ways so that sinners will turn back to You.

218. Deliver me from the guilt of bloodshed, O God. You who are God my Savior, and my tongue will sing of Your righteousness.

219. Open my lips, Lord, and my mouth to declare Your praise.

220. You do not delight in sacrifice, or I would bring it. You do not take pleasure in burnt offerings.

221. My sacrifice, O God is a broken spirit, a broken and contrite heart. You, God will not despise. (Psalm 51)

222. May it please You to prosper Zion, to build up the walls of Jerusalem, then You will delight in the sacrifices of the righteous, and burnt offerings offered whole, when bulls will be

offered on Your altar, in the Name of Jesus.

223. Lord, I am Yours. I live in You and You are in me.

224. Lord, remove all filth and sin from my life, in the Name of Jesus.

225. Father, change me from filthy garments, and I am washed by the washing of the water, by the Word. I put on the garments of praise and the clothes of righteousness, in Jesus' Name.

226. Lord, hide me in the cleft of the Rock, the Rock, which is Christ Jesus, as Your Glory fills this throne room with Your beauty and holiness and righteousness.

227. Cleanse me from all unrighteousness by the Blood of Jesus.

228. Thank You, God, for You are good, Your Mercy endures forever. (from Psalm 103).

229. Oh give thanks to the Lord of lords for His Mercy endures forever.

230. To Him alone doeth great wonders for his Mercy endureth forever.

231. To him that by wisdom made the heavens for his mercy endureth forever.

232. To him that stretched out the heavens above the waters, For his mercy endures forever.

233. To him that made great light, For his mercy endureth forever.

234. The sun to rule by day, For his mercy endureth forever,

235. And the moon and stars to rule by night, for his mercy endureth forever.

236. I praise You Lord, for You are worthy. King of kings, Lord of lords, King of Glory.

237. O that men would praise the Lord for His goodness, for His wonderful works to the children of men, for he

satisfies the longing soul and fills the hungry soul with goodness, such as sit in darkness and in the shadow of death, being bound in affliction and iron.

238. I praise You, Lord, for You have drawn me out of many waters. You have drawn me out of the miry clay, and you set my feet in a large place, in a green place, in the Name of Jesus.

239. Instead of the thorn and the briar, You've given me the fir tree and the myrtle tree.

240. Behold the voice of the Lord. The voice of rejoicing and salvation is in the tabernacles of the righteous.

241. The right hand of the Lord is valiant. The Lord's Right Hand is lifted high. Lord, You have saved me by Your Spirit, by Your Power, by Your Might, and by Your Righteous Right Hand.

242. I enter into Your courts of praise, and I bless Your Holy Name.

243. Lord of my strength and Lord of my salvation. I ascribe greatness to Your Name.

244. Your honor, Your Majesty, Righteous Judge.

245. to Him who sits on the throne and unto the Lamb, Alpha and Omega, the beginning and the ending, which is and was and which is to come. To the Almighty, blessings and power and honor to You forever. Amen.

246. Holy, holy, holy. You who was dead, and behold, is alive forevermore. Amen to Him with the keys of hell and death.

247. Thou art worthy, O Lord, to receive glory and honor and power. But that has created all things, and for Thy pleasure they are and were created.

248. I ask You, Mighty Father, judge in the matters concerning my life and wellbeing, in the Name of Jesus.

249. I pray that you pass upon them the judgment of Your consuming Fire, because that is what Your Word has said, that my God is a consuming Fire.

250. Let them be judged according to the standard of Your righteousness and of Your Fire, in the Name of Jesus, Amen.

251. Lord, You've blessed me mightily financially. You've given me the fruit of my labor.

252. You've blessed me coming in and going out.

253. You've made me prosperous, and You surround me as with a wall of Fire.

254. I am chosen of the Lord. I am in no wise cast down. Nothing can separate me from the Love of God that is in

Christ Jesus. Nothing can pluck me out of Your hand.

255. I am not a candidate to be stolen from, ripped off or robbed, in the Name of Jesus.

256. I belong to the Lord Jesus Christ. Angels of God surround me so that no evil comes near me, in the Name of Jesus.

257. No evil comes near my house or anything over which I have stewardship, in Jesus' Name.

258. The Lord keeps watch over my life, and over my house so that no evil befalls me, in the Name of Jesus.

259. I am the head only and not the tail. I am above only and not beneath.

260. I am the righteousness of God, in Christ Jesus.

261. I am not a man walking from Jerusalem to Jericho. I am not a

candidate to fall among some thieves.
I am not a candidate for thievery.

262. Judas is not invited into my life, my
business, my household. The devil
must take his hands off all things that
pertain to me, that pertain to my life
and to my godliness, in the Name of
Jesus.

263. Because of my tithes and offerings,
the devourer has no place in my life.
Lord Jesus, rebuke him forever from
my finances, in the Name of Jesus.

264. The thief cometh not but to steal, kill,
and destroy. But Jesus came that I
may have life and have it more
abundantly, and the devil is
trespassing in my life and territory.
Lord Jesus, rebuke him, in the Name
of Jesus.

265. Lord, return back to me everything
stolen, including time and territory, in
the Name of Jesus.

266. Therefore, the devil is not in any covenant with myself and Christ, nor can he be and nor can he be in any covenant between us.

267. The devil is trespassing on God's property and putting his hands on God's property--, that's me and the things that belong to my peace. He must be stopped, and he must recompense me for all loss, all losses, in the Name of Jesus.

268. I'm not a candidate for the bread of sorrow or the waters of affliction, in Jesus' Name.

269. The devil has no right to steal, kill or destroy anything in my life, any part of my life or any part of me, because I am in Christ.

270. I'm protected by the power of Christ, by the Blood of the Lamb.

271. No weapon formed against me shall prosper, in the Name of Jesus.

272. I ask You, Lord, have Mercy on me and judge the enemy of our souls and of my body, in the Name of Jesus.

273. Lord, judge whether infirmity or anything the enemy has inflicted upon me can remain in my body, in the Name of Jesus.

274. Lord, loose me from this infirmity, from this disease, this disorder, this pain, every sickness, and every symptom, and imbalance, in the Name of Jesus.

275. Lord, judge whether this loss, insufficiency, lack or poverty can remain in my life, in the Name of Jesus.

276. Lord, loose me fully from the Curse of the Law since Jesus has already died for me, in the Name of Jesus.

277. Lord, loose me from all loss, insufficiency, lack, or poverty, in the Name of Jesus.

278. Lord, I ask You to judge every witchcraft curse that the devil has fired against me, in the Name of Jesus, because there is no enchantment against Jacob.

279. I am the seed of Abraham, and I decree today that there is no enchantment of darkness, against Jacob. No power of hell can work against me. All their works are frustrated, and their works are rendered useless, in Jesus' Name.

280. I decree that the Fire of the Holy Spirit will consume every plan of the devil today, in the Name of Jesus.

281. I am favored on all sides; my cup runs over with goodness, in the Name of Jesus.

282. I sing Your praise, O Lord. For You have made the Earth Your footstool; and You have made me glad.

283. I sing Your praise, O Lord, because you are the King that can decree a thing, and it must be fulfilled.

284. I sing Your praise, mighty King, whose Glory no one can stand.

285. I've never seen the righteous forsaken Lord or their seed big bread. And therefore, my beloved, I am steadfast. Lord, make me steadfast, and I'm unmovable, always abounding in the work of the Lord.

286. Lord, I declare that my labor is not in vain, in the Name of Jesus.

287. Lord, in the Name of Jesus, Holy Father, let it be known today that I stand before Your Throne requiring judgment to be done for me according to the standard of Your Word and Your righteousness.

288. Lord, it is contrary to Your Word for me to labor without a reward. And there's also, contrary to the standard

of Your Word, for me to be laboring and with nothing to show for it.

289. But I plead my case before You at Your Throne, and I ask that in righteousness You judge this matter.

290. I pray also that you would judge every *spirit* behind all of my labor, yet having little to nothing to show for it, in the Name of Jesus.

291. I declare my righteous Father that my labor will be rewarded. Everything I do in life will have something to show for it. I will no longer labor in vain, in the Name of Jesus.

292. I declare that my labor shall be productive and it is blessed. So shall it be, in the Name of Jesus, Amen.

293. Lord, You give power to get wealth, power to receive wealth. The devil has no authority in that power, in the Name of Jesus.

294. Lord, You give Grace to receive wealth, to receive inheritance and

spoils from Your treasury. And, Grace is a power.

295. Your Word says that when the enemy is caught, he shall restore sevenfold. Even if we empty the enemy's storehouse, he still owes and he must pay, in the Name of Jesus

296. When the enemy is found out, he must restore, He must repay. And here's the enemy of Your people, Lord. Here he is, He's found out. He's already here, standing at Your Throne, accusing mankind day and night. Here he is.

297. I have found him going to and fro in the Earth, and now he's standing accusing the brethren.

298. Lord, I plead the Blood of Jesus over my life, and I plead Mercy and I counter accuse him as the Thief.

299. The accuser of the brethren is the one that attacked my health. He is the one

that attacked my finances and stole from me.

300. He is the one that delayed my blessings, and I require and request restoration. I request recompense. I request reparations, and restitution, in the Name of Jesus.

301. Father, in the Name of Jesus, I request provision, spoils of 7 times, sevenfold restoration even if we have to spoil the strong man's house.

302. Where the devil has attacked my finances and causes lack and insufficiency, debt or poverty, Lord, intervene, in the Name of Jesus.

303. Because when he is found, he must restore sevenfold and give, even if he has to give all the substance of his house, he must restore sevenfold.

304. By faith in Jesus Christ, I command and demand that the devil put back what he stole, in the Name of Jesus.

305. Lord, You said in Your Word, "Owe, no man anything but to love them."

306. And You said in Your Word that we should be lenders only and not borrowers, that we shall lend to many nations.

307. Lord, You said in Your Word that there should be abundance and no lack, and that those who love the Lord shall lack no good thing.

308. The Lord is my shepherd; I shall not want. I do not want, I do not lack for any good thing, nothing that pertains to life and to godliness.

309. Lord, as I have repented for robbing You and any person--, any man, any woman, any person, and repenting of hurting any man, any woman, any person, and I repent of any type of attack against any person, in the Name of Jesus.

310. I plead the Blood of Jesus and Lord, You love justice and You hate a false balance.

311. My being robbed of anything, anything good, anything given to me by You is unacceptable; it is a false balance. Balance me, Lord, in the Name of Jesus.

312. My being robbed of any inheritance is an abomination and unacceptable. It is counter to the Word. Because we should not even sell an inheritance, much less let it be stolen from us. Jesus died, that I may have life and have it more abundantly, and that is inheritance, because a man died.

313. Lord, You are the God of More Than Enough, El Shaddai. And I should have more than enough, because not having enough is under the Curse of the Law, and I'm redeemed from the Curse of the Law by Jesus Christ. And I must receive restitution and

also be restored, in the Name of Jesus.

314. I must be restored sevenfold, unless the depth of the enemy's evil is so deep, that I should receive more.

If Cain shall be avenged sevenfold, truly Lamech seventy and sevenfold. (Genesis 4:24)

315. Lord, bind the strongman, dislodge him from my gates and spoil his storehouse, in the Name of Jesus.

316. Lord, You said that You give us power to get wealth. Lord, also give me power to *receive* 7 times recompense and Wisdom to honor You in tithes and offerings once I receive it, in the Name of Jesus.

317. If the first fruit be holy, if the lump is also holy, and if the root be holy, so are the branches.

318. Lord, give Wisdom and obedience, so I may honor You in first fruits so that the lump is holy, in the Name of Jesus.

319. I will sanctify all my gains to the Lord my God and Maker of Heaven and Earth, in the Name of Jesus.

320. Thank You, Lord, that You hear and honor my prayers and petitions, in the Name of Jesus.

321. You are the Mighty God, the Righteous Judge, and You judge by justice.

322. Lord, please restore your servant to wholeness, even to overflowing, judging without delay in Your Mercy toward Your servant, in the Name of Jesus. Amen. Amen.

Tear Them Up

Then I turned, and lifted up mine eyes,
and looked, and behold a flying roll.

And he said unto me, What seest thou?
And I answered, I see a flying roll; the
length thereof *is* twenty cubits, and the
breadth thereof ten cubits.

Then said he unto me, This *is* the curse
that goeth forth over the face of the
whole earth: for every one that stealeth
shall be cut off *as* on this side according
to it; and every one that sweareth shall
be cut off *as* on that side according to it.

I will bring it forth, saith the LORD of
hosts, and it shall enter into the house of
the thief, and into the house of him that
sweareth falsely by my name: and it
shall remain in the midst of his house,
and shall consume it with the timber

thereof and the stones
thereof. (Zechariah 5:1-4)

323. Lord, send the Flying Scroll into the house of the thief and execute righteous judgment on that house and that thief, in the Name of Jesus. (X3)

324. Every thief that came in falsely pretending to be of God and they were not of God, receive the judgement of the Lord that I am calling for this day in the Name of Jesus. (X3)

325. Lord, judge by Your righteousness and execute with Your Rod of Iron, in the Name of Jesus.

326. To the only wise God our Saviour, be glory and majesty, dominion and power, both now and ever. Amen. (Jude 25)

327. Thank You, Lord, for hearing these prayers, I count it as done because You are Faithful, in the Name of Jesus.

328. I seal these words, prayers, decrees, declarations across every dimension, realm, era, timeline, past, present and future to infinity. I seal them with the Blood of Jesus and the Holy Spirit of Promise.

329. Every retaliation against these words, prayers, decrees, declarations, or against the speaker, the reader, the listener or anyone who prays these prayers at any time in the future, let that retaliation backfire with reverb against the evil perpetrator to infinity, without Mercy, in the Name of Jesus Christ.

Amen.

Book Recommendations:

AMONG SOME THIEVES

AMONG SOME THIEVES
https://a.co/d/dkYT4ZV

Thieves of the Darkness, a four-book series, **The Devourers, The Wasters, The Swallowers, The Emptiers** https://a.co/d/8yjIxfH

Here Come the Horns – for more on Divine Carpenters and Flying Scrolls. https://a.co/d/cVOfZrl

The Power to Get Wealth https://a.co/d/gOsILJ6

The spirit of poverty https://a.co/d/9U9M41U

Dear Reader:

Thank you for acquiring and reading this book. I pray it will inspire righteous indignation in you about being ripped off and cause you to pursue the thief and recover all that has been stolen from you, for life, purpose, and destiny, to the praise of God's Glory.

In Jesus' Name,

Amen.

Dr. Marlene Miles

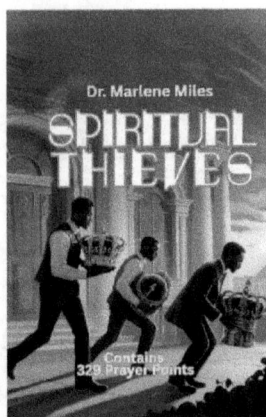

Prayerbooks by this author

While most books by this author have prayer points either throughout the book or at the end, there are some books that are only prayers. You just open up the book and pray.

Prayers Against Barrenness: *For Success in Business and Life*

Fruit of the Womb: *Prayers Against Barrenness*

Beauty Curses, *Warfare Prayers Against*
https://a.co/d/5Xlc20M

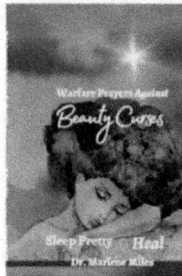

Courts of Marriage: Prayers for Marriage in the Courts of Heaven
(prayerbook) https://a.co/d/cNAdgAq

Courtroom Warfare @ Midnight
(prayerbook) https://a.co/d/5fc7Qdp

Demonic Cobwebs *(prayerbook)*
https://a.co/d/fp9Oa2H

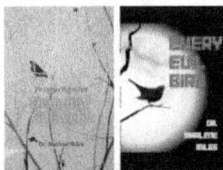

Every Evil Bird https://a.co/d/hF1kh1O

Gates of Thanksgiving

Spirits of Death, Hell & the Grave, Pass Over Me and My House

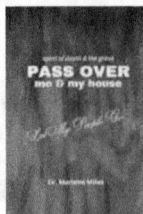

Throne of Grace: Courtroom Prayer

Warfare Prayer Against Poverty
https://a.co/d/bZ61lYu

Other books by this author

AK: The Adventures of the Agape Kid

Already Married in the Spirit: *Why You May Not Be Married in the Natural*

AMONG SOME THIEVES
https://a.co/d/dkYT4ZV

Ancestral Powers

Anti-Marriage, *The Spirit of*

Backstabbers https://a.co/d/gi8iBxf

Barrenness, *Prayers Against*
https://a.co/d/feUltIs

Battlefield of Marriage, *The*

Beware of the Dog: Prayers Against Dogs in the Dream.

Bless Your Food: *Let the Dining Table be Undefiled*

Blindsided: *Has the Old Man Bewitched You?* https://a.co/d/5O2fLLR

Break Free from Collective Captivity

Broken Spirits & Dry Bones

By Means of a Whorish Father

Casting Down Imaginations

Churchzilla, The Wanna-Be, Supposed-to-be Bride of Christ

Demonic Cobwebs (prayerbook)

Demonic Time Bombs

Demons Hate Questions

Devil Loves Trauma, *The*

Devil Weapons: Unforgiveness, Bitterness,...

The Devourers: Thieves of Darkness 2

Do Not Swear by the Moon

Don't Refuse Me, Lord (4 book series)
https://a.co/d/idP34LG

Dream Defilement

The Emptiers: *Thieves of Darkness, 1*
https://a.co/d/5I4n5mc

Evil Touch

Failed Assignment

Fantasy Spirit Spouse
https://a.co/d/hW7oYbX

FAT Demons (The): *Breaking Demonic Curses* https://a.co/d/4kP8wV1

The Fold (5-book series)

- The Fold (Book 1)
- Name Your Seed (Book 2)
- The Poor Attitudes of Money (3)
- Do Not Orphan Your Seed (4)
- For the Sake of the Gospel (5)
- My Sowing Journal

Gang Ups: Touch Not God's Anointed

Getting Rid of Evil Spiritual Food

https://a.co/d/i2L3WYQ

got HEALING? Verses for Life

got LOVE? Verses for Life

got HOPE? Verses for Life

got money? https://a.co/d/g2av41N

Here Come the Horns: *Skilled to Destroy*
https://a.co/d/cZiNnkP

Hidden Sins: Hidden Iniquity

https://a.co/d/4Mth0wa

How to Dental Assist

How to Dental Assist2: Be Productive, Not Wasteful

How to STOP Being a Blind Witch or Warlock

I Take It Back

Legacy

Let Me Have A Dollar's Worth
https://a.co/d/h8F8XgE

Level the Playing Field

Living for the NOW of God

Lose My Location
https://a.co/d/crD6mV9

Love Breaks Your Heart

Made Perfect In Love

Mammon https://a.co/d/29yhMG7

Man Safari, *The*

Marriage Ed. Rules of Engagement &
Marriage

Made Perfect in Love

Money Hunters: Beware of Those

Money on the Altar https://a.co/d/4EqJ2Nr

Mulberry Tree, *The*
https://a.co/d/9nR9rRb

Motherboard (The) - *Soul Prosperity
Series*

Name Your Seed

Occupy: *Until I Return*
https://a.co/d/bZ7ztUy

Plantation Souls

Players Gonna Play

<u>Portals</u>: Shut the Front Door: Prayers to Close Evil Portals.

Power Money: Nine Times the Tithe

https://a.co/d/gRt41gy

The Power of Wealth *(forthcoming)*

Powers Above

The Robe, Part 1, The Lessons of Joseph

The Robe, Part II, The Lessons of Joseph

Seasons of Grief

Seasons of Waiting

Seasons of War

Second Marriage, Third--, *Any Marriage*

https://a.co/d/6m6GN4N

Seducing Spirits: Idolatry & Whoredoms

https://a.co/d/4Jq4WEs

Shut the Front Door: *Prayers to Close Portals* https://a.co/d/cH4TWJj

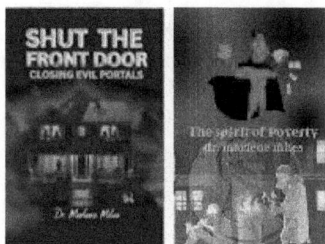

Sift You Like Wheat

Six Men Short: What Has Happened to all the Men?

Soul Prosperity soul prosperity series 3

https://a.co/d/5p8YvCN

Souls Captivity soul prosperity series 2

The Spirit of Anti-Marriage

The Spirit of Poverty
https://a.co/d/abV2o2e

StarStruck- Triangular Power series.

SUNBLOCK- Triangular Power series.

The Swallowers: *Thieves of Darkness*, 3

Take It Back

This Is NOT That: How to Keep Demons from Coming at You

Time Is of the Essence

Too Many Wives: *Why You Have Lady Problems*

Tormenting Spirits
https://a.co/d/dAogEJf

Toxic Souls

Triangular Power *(series)*

- Powers Above
- SUNBLOCK
- Do Not Swear by the Moon
- STARSTRUCK

Unbreak My Heart: *Don't Let Me Die*

Uncontested Doom

Unguarded Hours, *The*

Unseen Life, *The* (forthcoming)

Upgrade: How to Get Out of Survival Mode

- Toxic Souls (Book 2 of series)
- Legacy (Book 3 of series)

The Wasters: *Thieves of Darkness,* Bk 2
https://a.co/d/bUvI9Jo

What Have You to Declare? What Do You Have With You from Where You've Been?

When I Was A Child, *I Prayed As a Child*

When the Devourer is Rebuked

https://a.co/d/1HVv8oq

The Wilderness Romance *(series)* This series is about conducting a Godly relationship and marriage with someone who is a Wilderness person. It is about how to recognize it and navigate through it. These books are about how not to get caught up in such.

- *The Social Wilderness*
- *The Sexual Wilderness*
- *The Spiritual Wilderness*

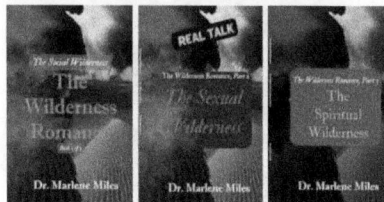

Other Series

The Fold (a series on Godly finances)

https://a.co/d/4hz3unj

Soul Prosperity Series

https://a.co/d/bz2M42q

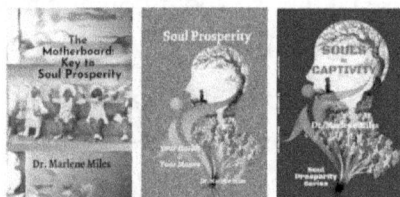

Spirit Spouse books

https://a.co/d/9VehDSo

https://a.co/d/97sKOwm

Battlefield of Marriage, The

https://a.co/d/eUDzizO

Players Gonna Play

https://a.co/d/2hzGw3N

Sent Spirit Spouse (can someone send you a spirit spouse? This book is not yet released.)

Matters of the Heart

Made Perfect in Love
https://a.co/d/7OMQW3O

Love Breaks Your Heart
https://a.co/d/4KvuQLZ

Unbreak My Heart
https://a.co/d/84ceZ6M

Broken Spirits & Dry Bones
https://a.co/d/e6iedNP

Thieves of Darkness series

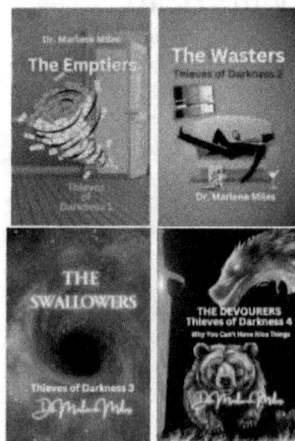

The Emptiers https://a.co/d/heio0dO

The Wasters https://a.co/d/5TG1iNQ

The Swallowers
https://a.co/d/1jWhM6G

The Devourers: Why We Can't Have Nice
Things https://a.co/d/87Tejbf

Triangular Powers https://a.co/d/aUCjAWC

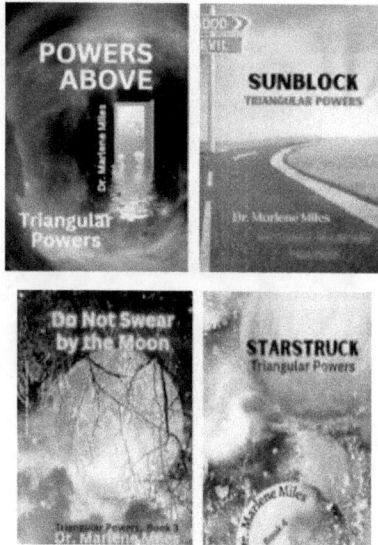

Upgrade (series) *How to Get Out of Survival Mode* https://a.co/d/aTERhXO

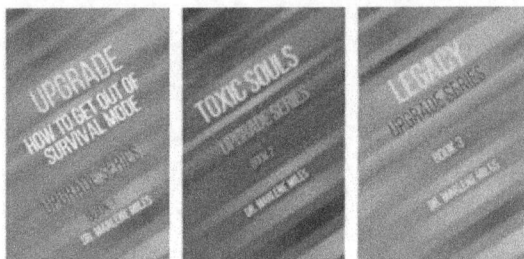

www.ingramcontent.com/pod-product-compliance
Lightning Source LLC
LaVergne TN
LVHW021357080426
835508LV00020B/2318